Contents

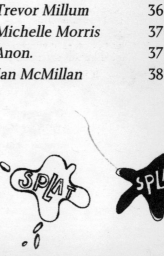

A Poem Stupid

The reading session's at an end and
all the class are quiet
Here's a wicked reading trick . . . if you dare to try it.

When asked, 'What are you reading?'
Put your teacher in a rage
As you pronounce the title
At the top of this page.

John Coldwell

Poem for a New Teacher

Welcome to the school, Miss.
We're The Class From Hell—
A wild, unruly mob which
Nobody can quell,
The kind of pupils other schools
Would certainly expel.

So come in, Miss. Excuse the mess,
The racket and the smell.
It's dingy in this classroom.
It's like a prison cell.
And some of us say that you won't stay
For long . . . but who can tell?

The cross on the floor records where
Our last teacher fell.
They say that someone tripped her up.
You should've heard her yell.
Anyway, they took away
A babbling, burnt-out shell

Who'd never dared to make us work,
Knowing we'd just rebel.
So most of us can't read or write
And none of us can spell.
But now they've sent us you, Miss.
You're the new personnel.

So come on in and meet us, Miss.
We really wish you well.
We hope you like a challenge, Miss,
Cos we're The Class From Hell.
We've got a lot of time to kill . . .
It's *hours* till the bell.

Nick Toczek

On and on . . .

Is a well-wisher someone
who wishes at a well?

Is a bad-speller one
who casts a wicked spell?

Is a shop-lifter a giant
who goes around lifting shops?

Is a pop singer someone
who sings and then pops?

Is a pot-holer a gunman
who shoots holes at pots?

Does a baby-sitter really
sit on tiny tots?

Is a light bulb a bulb
that is light as a feather?

Does an opera buff sing
in the altogether?

Does a pony trap trap ponies
going to the fair?

Is fire-hose stockings
that firemen wear?

Is a scratch team so itchy
it scratches?

When a bricklayer lays a brick
what hatches?

Is a sick bed a bed
that is feeling unwell?

Is a crime wave a criminal's
wave of farewell?

Is a bent copper a policeman
who has gone round the bend?

Is the bottom line the line
on your bottom? THE END

Roger McGough

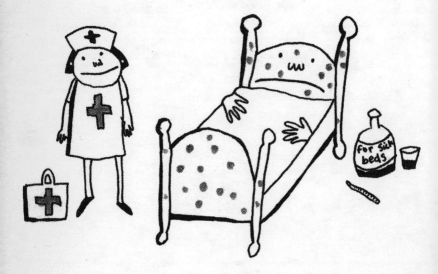

The Lesson

'Blether, blather, blah-blah, bosh.
Claptrap, humbug, poppycock, tosh.
Guff, flap-doodle, gas and gabble.
Hocus pocus, gibberish, babble.
Baloney, hooey, jabber, phew,
Stuff and nonsense, drivel, moo.
Rhubarb, rhubarb, rhubarb, banter.
Prattle, waffle, rave and ranter.
Rubbish, piffle, tommy-rot, guff,
Twaddle, bilge, bombast, bluff.

Thank you.'

Colin McNaughton

Sponsored Silence?

We said, Let's hold a sponsored swim
Let's hold a sponsored spell
A sponsored clap
A sponsored rap
A sponsored shout and yell.

Teacher said, They're great ideas
But they might provoke a riot
Too much noise
So, girls and boys,
Let's hold a sponsored q-u-i-e-t

We said, We understand your fears
We know just what you mean
So we held a vote
And the clear result
Was to hold a sponsored

SCREAM!

Roger Stevens

The Inspector Calls
(To be chanted at the end of term)

The room was cold and dingy,
And the windows far from clean.
No sand or clay or wall display,
Not a book was to be seen.

'I am sure you have a lot of fun,'
The School Inspector said
To all the little children
Who sat in silent dread.

'I am sure you have a lot of fun,'
The visitor repeated,
And the children nodded obediently,
'Oh yes, sir,' they all bleated.

But at the back sat Darren,
And he shook his little head.
'Well I don't have a lot of fun,'
The little Infant said.

'Of course you do!' the teacher snapped,
And fixed him with a glare.
'We're always having lots of fun!'
In a tone that said: 'Beware!'

But Darren shook his head again,
And they heard the Infant say:
'Well I do not remember it—
I must have been away that day!'

Gervase Phinn

Breaking up
(to be chanted towards the end of term)

This time next week I shall be
Out of this academy.

No more Latin, no more French
No more sitting on a hard school bench.

No more stale bread and butter
No more water from the gutter.

No more maggots in the spam
No more gobs of damson jam.

No more beetles in my tea
Making googly eyes at me.

If the master interferes
Knock him down and box his ears.

If he's not content with that
Fry his face in bacon fat.

If that does not serve him right
Blow him up with dynamite.

Anon.

Dinner Boy

I'm a lunch-time (munch-time)
naughty boy
in the lunch-time line
with all the other naughty boys
who've done a lunch-time crime.
Darren threw a yogurt cup and
Olly threw some cheese,
Thomas kicked at Michael
and Martin threw some peas.

We're standing in the naughty line
we're in it every day—
we miss our games and football
we miss PE and play . . .
We're the ones who do the awful things,
we're the ones who get sent out
for flicking bits of bacon
and stamping on a sprout.
We're the ones who can't talk quietly,
we're the ones who like to yell,
the ones who never listen,
the ones who miss the bell . . .

You'll see us by the teacher's room,
we stand there by the wall,
sometimes in the corridor
sometimes in the hall.
We have to say we're sorry
we hang our heads in shame,
but if you pass tomorrow
then we'll be here
—again!
YEAH!

Peter Dixon

A Remarkable Adventure

I was at my bedroom table
with a notebook open wide,
when a giant anaconda
started winding up my side,
I was filled with apprehension
and retreated down the stairs,
to be greeted at the bottom
by a dozen grizzly bears.

We tumultuously tussled
till I managed to get free,
then I saw, with trepidation,
there were tigers after me,
I could feel them growing closer,
I was quivering with fear,
then I blundered into quicksand
and began to disappear.

I was rescued by an eagle
that descended from the skies
to embrace me with its talons,
to my terror and surprise,
but that raptor lost its purchase
when a blizzard made me sneeze,
and it dropped me in a thicket
where I battered both my knees.

I was suddenly surrounded
by a troop of savage trolls,
who maliciously informed me
they would toast me over coals,
I was lucky to elude them
when they briefly looked away—
that's the reason why my homework
isn't here with me today.

Jack Prelutsky

Two Times Table!

Sussex way of counting sheep: in pairs.
With thanks to Paul Wakeham-Dawson.

Onerum (2)

Twoerum (4)

Cockerum (6)

Quertherum (8)

Shitherum (10)

Shatherum (12)

Wineberry (14)

Wagtail (16)

Tarrydiddle (18)

Den (20)

Anon.

Learning to Count?

Cumbrian way of counting sheep: one to twenty.

Yan, tan, tether, mether, pimp.
Sether, hether, hother, dother, dick.
Yan dick, tan dick, tether dick, mether dick, bumfit.
Yan bumfit, tan bumfit, tether bumfit, mether bumfit,
gigot.

Anon.

The wrong words

We like to sing the wrong words
to Christmas Carols . . .

We three kings of Orient are,
One in a taxi, one in a car . . .

It drives our music teacher barmy,
his face turns red as a holly berry,
his forehead creases,
his eyes bulge.
It looks as if the top of his head
is about to lift like a saucepan lid
as he boils over . . .

His anger spills out
in an almighty shout . . .

'NO,' he roars . . .

'If you do that once more
I'll give you the kind of Christmas gift
you won't forget in a hurry . . .'

So we sing . . .
  . . .*most highly flavoured lady . . .*

'IT'S FAVOURED,' he screams,
'NOT FLAVOURED . . .

So we all went completely quiet, then broke the eerie hush
with a rattle of dropped rulers, followed by a furious rush
of totally stupid questions, sniggers and rude squealing—
and at the bell, we could tell our marks were through the ceiling.

Our rivals, 3b, did quite well, but we won by several feet.
They came, they saw, they measured and admitted defeat,
so we're still the school champions, no doubt of it at all—
we're the class who drove their teacher
furthest up the wall!

Dave Calder

The Pet wig

Our teacher has a pet wig,
Nobody knows its name,
It clings to his baldy head
And looks extremely tame.

It's very calm and patient.
When dogs are on the prowl
It pretends it cannot hear the way
They clear their throats and growl.

It comes from a far-off land
(Or so we like to think),
A strange, endangered species
That's just about extinct.

After school he takes it off
And offers it some milk.
He strokes it extra gently
(Its fur is smooth as silk).

And in his lonely room at night
When he decides to retire,
He lays the wig quite carefully
On a blanket near the fire,

Where after a long day clinging
It rests content and purring.

Brian Patten

According to My Mood

I have poetic **licence,** i WriTe thE way i waNt.
i *drop* my **full stops** where *i* like . . .
MY CAPITAL LeteRs go where I liKE,
i order from MY PeN, i verse **the way** i like
    (**i do** *my spelling write*)
According to My mood.
i HAve poetic **licence,**
i put my **commers** where I like,,((()).
(((my brackets *are* **write**((
I REPEAT WHen i likE.
i **can't go rOng.**
i *look* and **i.c.**
It's **rite.**
I I REPEAT WHen i likE. **i** have
poetic **licence!**
d**O**n't question me???

Benjamin Zephaniah

A Student's Prayer

Now I lay me down to rest,
I pray I pass tomorrow's test.
If I should die before I wake,
That's one less test I'll have
   to take.

Anon.

Today

Today I will not live up to my potential.
Today I will not relate well to my peer group.
Today I will not contribute in class.
    I will not volunteer one thing.
Today I will not strive to do better.
Today I will not achieve or adjust or grow enriched
    or get involved.
I will not put up my hand even if the teacher is wrong
    and I can prove it.

Today I might eat the eraser off my pencil.
I'll look at the clouds.
I'll be late.
I don't think I'll wash.

I need a rest.

Jean Little

Don't do as I do—Do as I say!

'Sit up straight!'
She slouched.
'You don't have to shout!'
She yelled.
'I won't tell you again!'
She told us again.

'I shouldn't need to explain!'
She explained.
'This work is untidy,'
She scribbled.
'I won't tell you again!'
She told us again.

And again.

Trevor Millum

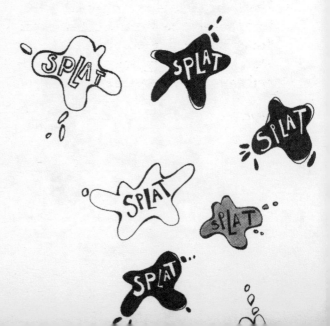

Is your Schoolteacher Such an old bag?

Is your schoolteacher such an old bag,
Does she pester and wheedle and nag?
And have you a hunch
When the bell goes for lunch
That she runs to the loo for a fag?

Michelle Morris

There was a young lady...

There was a young lady of Poole
Who thought she would set up a school;
But all she could teach
Was nine parts of speech
And how to make gooseberry fool.

Anon.

Teacher wind-up poem

Hey (insert name of teacher)!
Hey (insert name of teacher)!
Hello!

Hey (insert name of teacher)!
My (insert name of elderly relative) had hair like that!
We told (insert name of elderly relative) it looked lovely!
Just like in the old days!

Hey (insert name of teacher)!
My (insert name of pet) has eyes like that!
We told (insert name of elderly relative) it was
    almost human!
Just like a real person!

Hey (insert name of teacher)!
We saw (insert name of another teacher who your
    teacher fancies)
In town with (insert name of another teacher on the staff)!
They were laughing at something!

Hey (insert name of teacher)!
Hey (insert name of teacher)!
Hey (insert name of teacher)!
Goodbye!

Ian McMillan

Teachers, Beware!

I'm the boy at the back
Who mutters and mumbles;
Who, at the word 'Homework',
Grimaces, grumbles;
Who laughs long and loud
When the class-teacher stumbles;
Who, in the dark playground,
Loves real rough-and-tumbles;
Who makes odd rude noises;
Whose tum rudely rumbles.
I'm fierce and I'm foul,
An oik whom none humbles.
I'm the bad boy at the back!
Yes!
I'm the bad boy at the back!

John Kitching

Our teacher

Our teacher's got a bunion
And a face like a pickled onion
A nose like a squashed tomato
And legs like two sticks.

Anon.

Billy McBone

Billy McBone
Had a mind of his own,
Which he mostly kept under his hat.
The teachers all thought
That he couldn't be taught,
But Bill didn't seem to mind that.

Billy McBone
Had a mind of his own,
Which the teachers had searched for
    for years.
Trying test after test,
They still never guessed
It was hidden between his ears.

Billy McBone
Had a mind of his own,
Which only his friends ever saw.
When the teacher said, 'Bill,
Whereabouts is Brazil?'
He just shuffled and stared at the floor.

Billy McBone
Had a mind of his own,
Which he kept under lock
    and key.
While the teachers in vain
Tried to burgle his brain,
Bill's thoughts were off
    wandering free.

Allan Ahlberg

God Made Bees

God made bees
Bees make honey
We do the work
But teachers get the money.

Anon.

where's That?

Geography is never for me
And causes my teachers to sigh.
I certainly know
That Holland's quite low,
Mount Everest is terribly high.

The rivers that wind
I never can find
Whenever I'm put to the test.
Now Scotland's up north
With the Firth of the Forth,
America's somewhere out west.

I'm puzzled and dull
When searching for Hull
And cities like Rio and Rome.
My teacher will fret
That I can't find Tibet
But at least I can find
   my way home.

Max Fatchen

Stinker

Poor old Stinker's dead and gone
We'll see his face no more
For what he thought was H_2O
Was H_2SO_4.

Anon.

Arithmetic

Two wrongs don't make a right.
So says my teacher, Mr Brill.
Two wrongs don't make a right,
   say I.
But maybe four wrongs will.

Judith Viorst

Dumb Insolence

I'm big for ten years old
Maybe that's why they get at me

Teachers, parents, cops
Always getting at me

When they get at me

I don't hit em
They can do you for that

I don't swear at em
They can do you for that

I stick my hands in my pockets
And stare at them

And while I stare at them
I think about sick

They call it dumb insolence

They don't like it
But they can't do you for it

Adrian Mitchell

Inquisitiveness

Please, how does one spell *definite*?
Has it a double *f* in it?

Please, how old was Euripides?
And where are the Antipodes?

Please, where does one find phosphorus?
And how big is the Bosporus?

Please, why are you so furious?
Do tell me, I'm *so* curious.

Colin West

That's Impossible, Miss!

'Nothing is impossible!'
Said the teacher with a hiss.
'How about a cross-eyed
Cyclops, miss?'

Colin McNaughton

They Put Me in the Stupid Class

They put me in the stupid class
When history I did not pass.
But I'll show them,
Just wait and see—
I'll graduate with a degree
In economic management.
And then I'll run for president,
Where in a landslide I will win.

Then heads will roll and tails will spin.
I'll round up all my teachers fast
And put *them* in the stupid class.

Douglas Florian

waste

Our governess—would you believe
It?—drowned herself on Christmas Eve!
This was a waste, as, anyway,
It would have been a holiday.

Harry Graham

I Love to Do My Homework

I love to do my homework,
It makes me feel so good.
I love to do exactly
As my teacher says I should.

I love to do my homework,
I never miss a day.
I even love the men in white
Who are taking me away.

Anon.

Homework

I love my school so very much
that I'm taking it home
bit by bit in my bag.

My mother says it's stealing
but I don't think it's stealing,
it's really just collecting.

I've got three bricks
and a desk so far.

The bricks were easy
but the desk was hard.

Ian McMillan

I Dreamt I Took Over . . .

I dreamt I took over my secondary school . . .

I sacked the Headteacher for breaking the rules,
Kept the teachers outside during break in the cold
And took all their cigarettes. 'You're really too old
To be smoking. Haven't you learnt yet?' I said.
'Learn to say no. You're too easily led!'

I told them to stop laughing and messing about,
'The staff room's a cesspit. Get it cleaned out!
And, Deputy, don't drive that car like a bat out of hell;
Wait in the car park till the end of school bell.'
I called in the matron and checked them for nits,
Tested their eyes and then tested their wits:
Gave them all an IQ test, kept them in after school—
Made them read out their answers so they'd each feel a fool.

Several were sent home to change shirts or their ties
Or put on dull dresses of more suitable size.
I gave lots of homework, which I didn't explain;
They put up their hands and asked questions in vain.
'You should have been listening,' I said with a smile,
'Hand in tomorrow. Now line up, single file!'
I ignored their excuses that they had to go out.
'Your work must come first,' I said with a shout.
'Reports will be issued at the end of the term.
If you've not shown improvement I'll have to be firm:
It may be the thumbscrews, it may be the rack . . .
I'm going to wake up now—but I'll be back!'

Trevor Millum

There was once a Student...

There was once a student named Bessor
Whose knowledge grew lessor and lessor.
It at last grew so small
He knew nothing at all
And today he's a college professor.

Anon.

The Crocodile

This is a Crocodile, my boy . . .
Or is it an Alligator? . . .
I've an excellent book that you'll enjoy
We can refer to later;

The Alligator . . . no, Crocodile
Is a purplish colour beneath.
Give it a tickle to make it smile
And let's count the number of teeth,

For the Croc (I think) has a row too few
Though the Gator can't wink its eye . . .

Ah!
    Now I can tell you which of the two
You have just been eaten by.

Michael Flanders

Teachers' Prayer

Let the children in our care
Clean their shoes and comb their hair;
Come to school on time—and neat,
Blow their noses, wipe their feet.
Let them, Lord, *not* eat in class
Or rush into the hall *en masse*.
Let them show some self-control;
Let them slow down; let them *stroll* !

Let the children in our charge
Not be violent or large;
Not be sick on the school-trip bus,
Not be cleverer than us;
Not be unwashed, loud or mad,
(With a six-foot mother or a seven-foot dad).
Let them, please, say 'drew' not 'drawed';
Let them *know the answers*, Lord!

Allan Ahlberg

Acknowledgements

We are grateful for permission to reproduce the following poems:

Allan Ahlberg: 'Billy McBone' and 'Teachers' Prayer' from *Heard it in the Playground* (Viking, 1989), copyright © Allan Ahlberg 1989, reprinted by permission of Penguin Books Ltd.
Max Fatchen: 'Where's That?' from *Peculiar Rhymes and Lunatic Lines* (Orchard Books, 1995), reprinted by permission of John Johnson (Authors' Agent) Ltd.
Michael Flanders: 'The Crocodile' from *Creatures Great and Small* (Dennis Dobson, 1964), reprinted by permission of the Flanders estate.
Douglas Florian: 'They Put Me in the Stupid Class' from *Bing Bang Boing* (Harcourt, 1994) copyright © 1994 by Douglas Florian, reprinted by permission of Harcourt. Inc.
Harry Graham: 'Waste' from *When Grandmama Fell Off the Boat: The Best of Harry Graham* (Methuen, 1986), reprinted by permission of Laura Dance.
Roger McGough: 'On and On' from *Lucky: A Book of Poems* (Viking, 1993), copyright © Roger McGough 1993, reprinted by permission of Penguin Books Ltd.
Colin McNaughton: 'The Lesson' from *There's An Awful Lot of Weirdos in Our Neighbourhood* (Walker Books, 1987), copyright © Colin McNaughton 1987, and 'That's Impossible, Miss!' from *Making Friends with Frankenstein* (Walker Books, 1993), copyright © Colin McNaughton 1993, reprinted by permission of Walker Books Ltd, London.
Adrian Mitchell: 'Dumb Insolence' from *Balloon Lagoon* (Orchard Books, 1999), copyright © Adrian Mitchell 1999, reprinted by permission of PFD on behalf of the author. Educational Health Warning! Adrian Mitchell asks that none of his poems are used in connection with any examinations whatsoever.
Brian Moses: 'The Wrong Words' from *Don't Look at Me in That Tone of Voice!* (Macmillan Children's Books, 1998).
Brian Patten: 'The Pet Wig' from *Thawing Frozen Frogs* (Viking, 1990), copyright © Brian Patten 1990, reprinted by permission of the author c/o Rogers, Coleridge & White Ltd, 20 Powis Mews, London W11 1JN.
Jack Prelutsky: 'A Remarkable Adventure' from *Something BIG has Been Here* (Heinemann Young Books, 1991), text copyright © Jack Prelutsky 1990, reprinted by permission of HarperCollins Publishers, USA.
Judith Viorst: 'Arithmetic' from *Sad Underwear* (Simon & Schuster, 1995), copyright © Judith Viorst, reprinted by permission of A. M. Heath & Co. Ltd on behalf of the author.